IF I WERE A... FISH

WRITTEN BY
CHARIS MATHER

WINDMILL BOOKS

Published in 2025 by Windmill Books,
an Imprint of Rosen Publishing
2544 Clinton St.
Buffalo, NY 14224

Written by:
Charis Mather

Edited by:
E.C. Andrews

Designed by:
Ker Ker Lee

Cataloging-in-Publication Data
Title: Fish / Charis Mather.
Description: Buffalo, NY : Windmill Books, 2025.
| Series: If I were a… | Includes glossary and index.
Identifiers: ISBN 9781538398104 (pbk.) |
ISBN 9781538398111 (library bound) |
ISBN 9781538398128 (ebook)
Subjects: LCSH: Fishes--Juvenile literature.
Classification: LCC QL617.2 M376 2025 |
DDC 597.156--dc23

Printed in the United States of America

CPSIA Compliance Information: Batch #CW25WM
For Further Information contact Rosen Publishing at 1-800-237-9932

Find us on

Photo Credits – Images are courtesy of Shutterstock.com. With thanks to Getty Images, Thinkstock Photo and iStockphoto.

Characters – yusufdemirci. Recurring images – Sachiko Nakai. Cover – Andrea Izzotti, Krzysztof Odziomek, Makabas, Vladimir Wrangel. 2–3 – Solarisys. 4–5 – panpilai paipa. 6–7 – Grigorev Mikhail, Volha Vasilevich, Vector Tradition. 8–9 – Beautiful landscape, Didier Barriere Doleac. 10–11 – Marben, AshtonEa, natchapohn. 12–13 – nicolasvoisin44, Kjersti Joergensen. 14–15 – Dwi Agung Sulistyo, I Wayan Sumatika, moj0j0. 16–17 – Lindsey Lu, Onusa Putapitak, Nsit. 18–19 – Vitaliy6447, Laura Dts, summer studio. 20–21 – Wirestock Creators, Daboost.

CONTENTS

Words that look like <u>this</u> can be found in the glossary on page 24.

FANTASTIC FISH

It must be fantastic to be a fish.

FISH ARE CREATURES THAT LIVE IN THE WATER. FISH HAVE GILLS AND FINS.

Some fish are famous for their fabulous colors. Some are famous for their spectacular swimming abilities.

If you were a fish, what would you be? Would you live in salty seas or freshwater ponds? Would you swim near the surface or down in the depths? There are thousands of fish to choose from!

GLASS CATFISH

Glass catfish are not quite invisible, but they are pretty close! Most of their body is see-through. Because of this, you can see a glass catfish's bones through its skin!

UP CLOSE, YOU CAN SEE A GLASS CATFISH'S HEART BEATING.

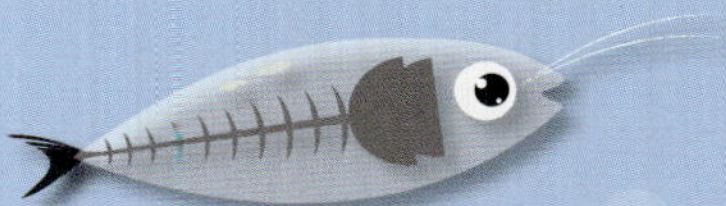

When glass catfish move in certain ways, they **shimmer** with rainbow colors. This may help them confuse other animals that want to eat them. It makes them look like flashes of light in the water.

EEL

I would be an eel so I could wiggle through the water.

Most fish swim using their fins. Eels do not have as many fins as most fish, so they swim by moving their long bodies up and down instead. They can even swim backwards!

To stay hidden while resting or hunting, some eels slither into small gaps between rocks or rocklike creatures called corals. When small creatures pass by, the eels dart out and catch their food.

LEAFY SEA DRAGON

Even though it looks like a plant, the leafy sea dragon is actually a fish. Its body has many leaflike parts that sway in the water. These are not used for swimming - they are used for camouflage.

Patches of seaweed, kelp, and seagrass are the perfect places for leafy sea dragons to hide. Leafy sea dragons blend into their surroundings, which makes it hard for other animals to spot them.

MANTA RAY

The largest kind of manta ray can grow to nearly 30 feet (9 m) long. That is the length of two cars! Manta rays keep their large bodies free of parasites by visiting areas full of parasite-eating fish.

Manta rays are not just known for their big bodies. They also have big brains! Manta rays are great problem solvers. They have excellent memories, which they use to find their way around the ocean.

MUDSKIPPER

Mudskippers are very unusual fish. They are amphibious, which means they can live in the water or on land. Thanks to their very strong fins and tails, mudskippers can walk, climb, and skip on land.

Mudskippers' eyes are on the top of their heads. They can move each eye separately to look for food in different directions. They blink a lot to keep their eyes from drying out.

MUDSKIPPERS ARE THE ONLY KIND OF FISH KNOWN TO BLINK.

WHALE SHARK

Whale sharks are the world's largest fish. This means that they need a lot of food to keep them going. However, whale sharks do not usually hunt like other sharks. They are filter feeders.

Whale sharks swim around with their mouths wide open. This helps them collect tiny ocean creatures to eat. Whale sharks travel about 5,000 miles (8,000 km) every year just to find enough food.

LIONFISH

Red stripes and long spines make lionfish easy to spot. However, not many creatures dare to hunt or even go near a lionfish. Lionfish spines are very venomous.

When hunting, lionfish make the most of their large fins. They spread them out and herd animals into small spaces. Then, the creatures have nowhere to escape, and the lionfish snap them up.

ARCHERFISH

Archerfish have one of the cleverest and most creative ways of catching food of any fish. They can squirt powerful jets of water into the air. These jets knock insects off branches and into the water.

I would be an archerfish! They have such good aim.

Archerfish need very good eyesight to hunt. They also have to be skilled enough to work out where to aim. Hitting small targets from different distances is not easy!

ARCHERFISH SPEND LOTS OF TIME NEAR THE SURFACE LOOKING FOR INSECTS.

WHAT WOULD YOU BE?

If I were a fish, I would be...

...as invisible as a glass catfish.

...as good at swimming as an eel.

...as well-camouflaged as a leafy sea dragon.

...as clever as a manta ray.

What would you be?

GLOSSARY

camouflage a way for animals to hide by looking like their surroundings

filter feeders animals that get food by taking in large amounts of water filled with small creatures, then pushing out the extra water

gills the body parts that some animals use to breathe underwater

herd to gather animals in one place

parasites creatures that live on or in another creature

shimmer to shine or sparkle with a gently flickering light

spines stiff, pointed spikes

surface the top layer of a body of water

venomous able to poison another animal through a bite or a scratch

INDEX